My R Words

Consultants

Ashley Bishop, Ed.D.
Sue Bishop, M.E.D.

Publishing Credits

Dona Herweck Rice, *Editor-in-Chief*

Robin Erickson, *Production Director*

Lee Aucoin, *Creative Director*

Sharon Coan, *Project Manager*

Jamey Acosta, *Editor*

Rachelle Cracchiolo, M.A.Ed., *Publisher*

Image Credits

cover Ljupco Smokovski/Shutterstock; p.2 Ljupco Smokovski/Shutterstock; p.3 Losevsky Pavel/Shutterstock; p.4 Roman Sigaev/Shutterstock; p.5 TRINACRIA PHOTO/Shutterstock; p.6 Pichugin Dmitry/Shutterstock; p.7 Cheryl E. Davis/Shutterstock; p.8 Vlue/Shutterstock; p.9 Baloncici/Shutterstock; p.10; back cover Pichugin Dmitry/Shutterstock

---

Teacher Created Materials

5301 Oceanus Drive
Huntington Beach, CA 92649-1030
http://www.tcmpub.com

ISBN 978-1-4333-2558-8

© 2012 Teacher Created Materials, Inc.
Printed in China

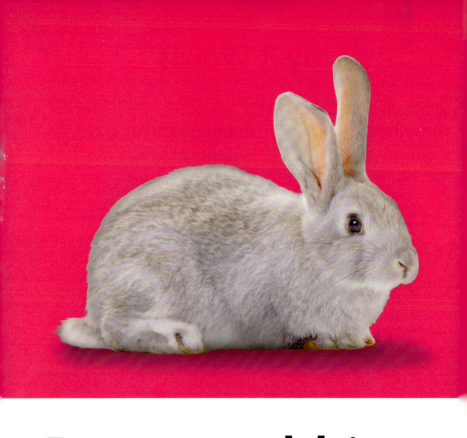

I see a rabbit.

I see a **radio**.

I see a raincoat.

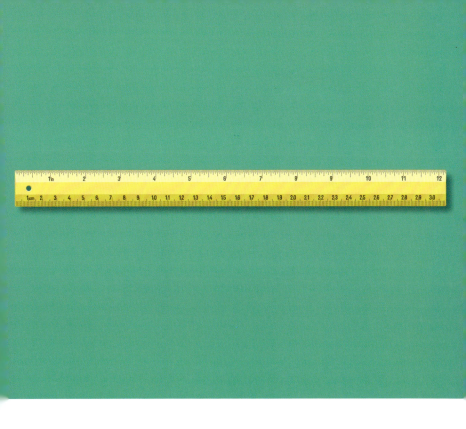

I see a **r**uler.

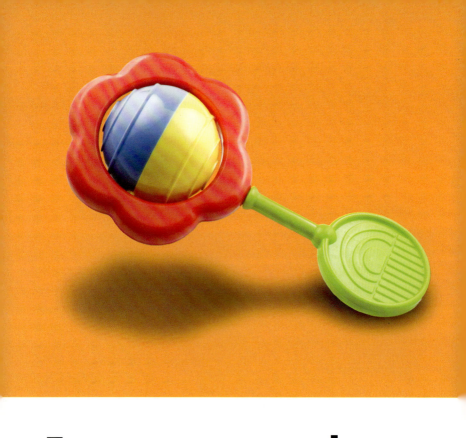

I see a **r**attle.

I see a rainbow.

I see a **r**ake.

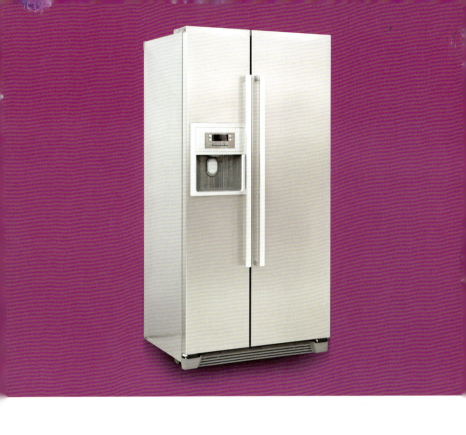

I see a refrigerator.

I see raisins.

Glossary

Sight Words
I　　see　　a

Activities

- Read the book aloud to your child, pointing to the *r* words as you say them. After reading each page, ask, "What do you see?"

- Tell your child that many times after it rains, a rainbow appears in the sky. Have your child draw a picture of a rainbow. Make sure to use the following colors: red, orange, yellow, green, blue, and purple.

- Help your child use a ruler to measure things around your home including the length and width of the refrigerator. Remind him or her that the words *ruler* and *refrigerator* begin with *r*.

- Make a rattle by using a container with a snap-on lid and paper to decorate the outside. Place dry beans or rice inside, close the lid, and let your child shake it. Encourage your child to say "r, r, r," as he or she shakes the rattle.

- Help your child think of a personally valuable word to represent the letter *r*, such as *respect*.